Meet the
JACKSONVILLE
JAGUARS

BY
ZACK BURGESS

NORWOODHOUSE 🏠 PRESS
CHICAGO, ILLINOIS

NORWOODHOUSE PRESS

P.O. Box 316598 • Chicago, Illinois 60631
For more information about Norwood House Press please visit our website at
www.norwoodhousepress.com or call 866-565-2900.

Photo Credits:
All photos courtesy of Associated Press, except for the following: Topps, Inc. (6, 11 top & middle),
Black Book Archives (7, 15, 18, 22), Donruss–Panini America (10 top, 11 bottom),
Sports Illustrated for Kids (10 bottom), Fleer Corp. (23).

Cover Photo: Phelan M. Ebenhack/Associated Press

The football memorabilia photographed for this book is part of the authors' collection. The collectibles used
for artistic background purposes in this series were manufactured by many different card companies—
including Bowman, Donruss, Fleer, Leaf, O-Pee-Chee, Pacific, Panini America, Philadelphia Chewing Gum,
Pinnacle, Pro Line, Pro Set, Score, Topps, and Upper Deck—as well as several food brands, including
Crane's, Hostess, Kellogg's, McDonald's and Post.

Designer: Ron Jaffe
Series Editors: Mike Kennedy and Mark Stewart
Project Management: Black Book Partners, LLC.
Editorial Production: Lisa Walsh

LIBRARY OF CONGRESS CATALOGING-IN-PUBLICATION DATA
Names: Burgess, Zack.
Title: Meet the Jacksonville Jaguars / by Zack Burgess.
Description: Chicago, Illinois : Norwood House Press, [2016] | Series: Big
    picture sports | Includes bibliographical references and index. |
    Audience: Grade: K to Grade 3.
Identifiers: LCCN 2015026328| ISBN 9781599537375 (Library Edition : alk.
    paper) | ISBN 9781603578400 (eBook)
Subjects: LCSH: Jacksonville Jaguars (Football team)--Miscellanea--Juvenile
    literature.
Classification: LCC GV956.J33 B87 2016 | DDC 796.332/640975912--dc23
LC record available at http://lccn.loc.gov/2015026328

288N—072016
Manufactured in the United States of America in North Mankato, Minnesota

CONTENTS

Words in **bold type** are defined on page 24.

The Jaguars are ready for action.

CALL ME A JAGUAR

Playing the Jacksonville Jaguars on their home turf can be like a trip to the jungle. It is very loud and scary. The Jaguars are like the big cats they are named after. They use speed and surprise to win. The "Jags" play hard every game from beginning to end.

TIME MACHINE

The Jaguars played their first season in the National Football League (NFL) in 1995. They almost reached the Super Bowl in their second season. The Jaguars built their team around players with great skill. Fred Taylor and **Maurice Jones-Drew** were two of the best.

Fred Taylor was one of the top running backs in team history.

The Jaguars' stadium is a great place to watch a game.

Best Seat in the House

The Jaguars' stadium is located on the St. John's River in northeast Florida. Football has been played in this area for more than 100 years. The Jaguars always have a chance to add to that history. This keeps the fans excited all game long.

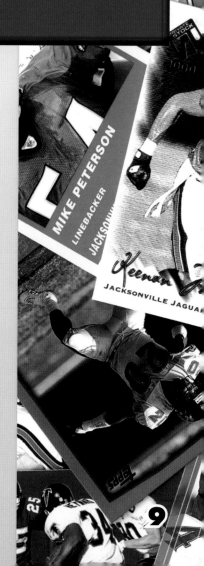

SHOE BOX

The trading cards on these pages show some of the best Jaguars ever.

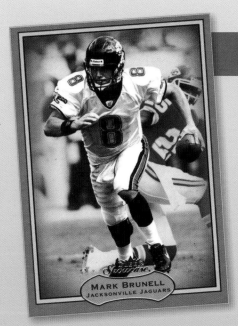

MARK BRUNELL

QUARTERBACK · 1995–2003

Mark was a confident passer with a strong arm. He set team records for passing yards and touchdowns.

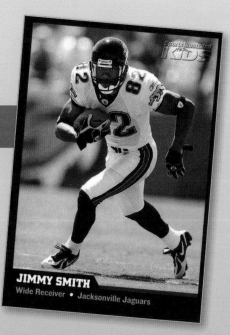

JIMMY SMITH

RECEIVER · 1995–2005

Jimmy had great speed and sure hands. He and Keenan McCardell were nicknamed "Thunder and Lightning."

FRED TAYLOR

RUNNING BACK · 1998-2008

Fred had an exciting mix of speed and power. He rushed for more than 1,000 yards seven times for the Jaguars.

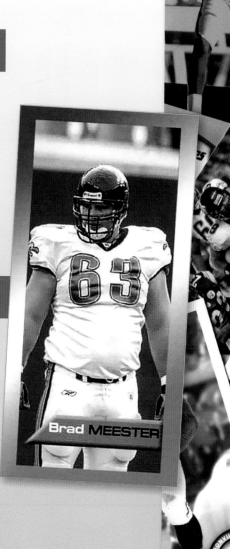

BRAD MEESTER

CENTER · 2000-2013

Brad was as tough as they come. He played 209 games for the Jaguars and started every one of them!

JOSH SCOBEE

KICKER · 2004-2014

Josh had a strong leg. He tied an NFL record by kicking three field goals of more than 50 yards in one game.

THE BIG PICTURE

Look at the two photos on page 13. Both appear to be the same. But they are not. There are three differences. Can you spot them?

Answers on page 23.

13

TRUE OR FALSE?

Maurice Jones-Drew was a star running back. Two of these facts about him are **TRUE**. One is **FALSE**. Do you know which is which?

1 Maurice led the NFL with 1,606 rushing yards in 2011.

2 Maurice was the shortest player in NFL history.

3 Maurice started just one game as a **rookie** but still scored 15 touchdowns.

14

Answer on page 23.

Maurice Jones-Drew loved playing for the Jaguars.

The Jaguars love to connect with their fans.

Go Jaguars, Go!

The Jaguars know how to connect with their fans. Before home games, fans form a "tunnel" for the players to run through. The stadium has zip lines and climbing walls. On hot days, fans can mist themselves in the Cool Zone.

ON THE MAP

Here is a look at where five Jaguars were born, along with a fun fact about each.

 TONY BOSELLI · MODESTO, CALIFORNIA
Tony was named **All-Pro** from 1997 to 1999.

 KEENAN McCARDELL · HOUSTON, TEXAS
Keenan had 499 catches in six seasons with the Jaguars.

 JOHN HENDERSON · NASHVILLE, TENNESSEE
John was the team's top **draft pick** in 2002.

 DAVID GARRARD · EAST ORANGE, NEW JERSEY
David played his best when the pressure was on.

 REGGIE WILLIAMS · LANDSTUHL, GERMANY
Reggie led the team with 10 touchdown catches in 2007.

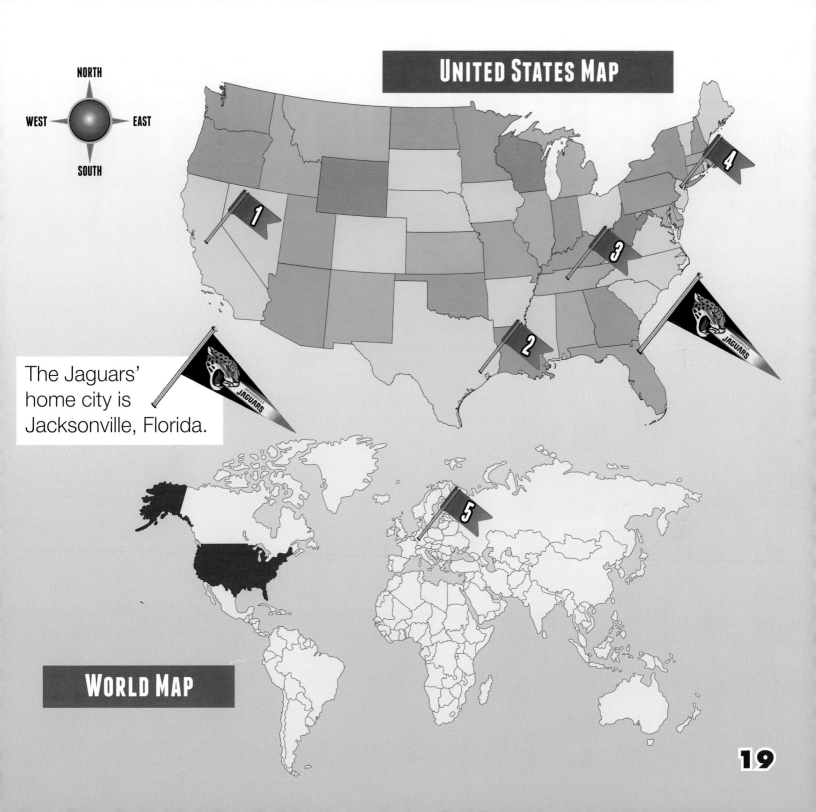

NORTH

WEST — EAST

SOUTH

1

4

3

2

The Jaguars' home city is Jacksonville, Florida.

5

WORLD MAP

19

HOME AND AWAY

Blake Bortles wears the Jaguars' home uniform.

Football teams wear different uniforms for home and away games. The main colors of the Jaguars are gold, white and a blue-green color called teal. They also use black.

T.J. Yeldon wears the Jaguars' away uniform.

The Jaguars' helmet looks black in the front and gold in the back. There is a gold jaguar head on each side. The big cat's tongue is teal!

WE WON!

The Jaguars played for the championship of the **American Football Conference** twice in their first five seasons. They relied on a great defense led by Kevin Hardy and Tony Brackens. Quarterback **Mark Brunell** was the leader of the offense.

RECORD BOOK

These Jaguars set team records.

TOUCHDOWN PASSES   RECORD

Season: Blake Bortles (2015)   35

Career: Mark Brunell   144

RUSHING YARDS   RECORD

Season: Maurice Jones-Drew (2011) 1,606

Career: Fred Taylor   11,271

FIELD GOALS   RECORD

Season: **Mike Hollis** (1997 & 1999)   31 ●——➤

Career: Josh Scobee   235

MIKE HOLLIS • K

FLEER TRADITION

ANSWERS FOR THE BIG PICTURE
    #5's helmet changed color, the football changed
to a basketball, and #76's socks changed color.

ANSWER FOR TRUE AND FALSE
    #2 is false. Maurice was not
the shortest player in the NFL.

Football Words

All-Pro
An honor given to the best NFL player at each position.

American Football Conference
One of two conferences of teams that make up the NFL.

Draft Pick
A player selected during the NFL's meeting each spring.

Rookie
A player in his first season.

Index

Photos are on **BOLD** numbered pages.

ABOUT THE AUTHOR

Zack Burgess has been writing about sports for more than 20 years. He has lived all over the country and interviewed lots of All-Pro football players, including Brett Favre, Eddie George, Jerome Bettis, Shannon Sharpe, and Rich Gannon. Zack was the first African American beat writer to cover Major League Baseball when he worked for the *Kansas City Star*.

ABOUT THE JAGUARS

Learn more at these websites:

www.jaguars.com • www.profootballhof.com

www.teamspiritextras.com/Overtime/html/jaguars.html